T for Tinkercad & C for Codeblock

This book is all about 3d modelling using code blocks, a new way of "scripting" the 3D model creation steps. The material is written to be more human while being technically accurate and useful. We use Tinkercad Codeblock for demonstration. It is a free web based software everyone can enjoy.

Table of Contents

Basic 3D concepts...3
Traditional 3D modelling VS codeblocks......................14
Project 1 - A basic car..23
Project 2 - A car with fancy features.........................33
Project 3 - Tire rim..39
Project 4 - Car body...54

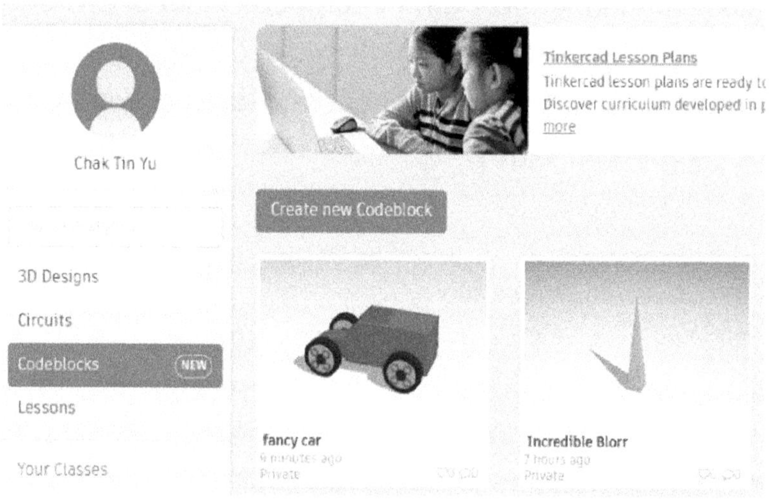

Basic 3D concepts

Before you start, it would be helpful to grab basic understanding on the various 3D concepts first. Even though our focus is on code block, you must know how 3D modelling works here.

A plane (aka work plane) is like a table top – it gives you a surface for working.

Things "on" a plane can be moved or scaled in multiple directions. Tinkercad has one such plane.

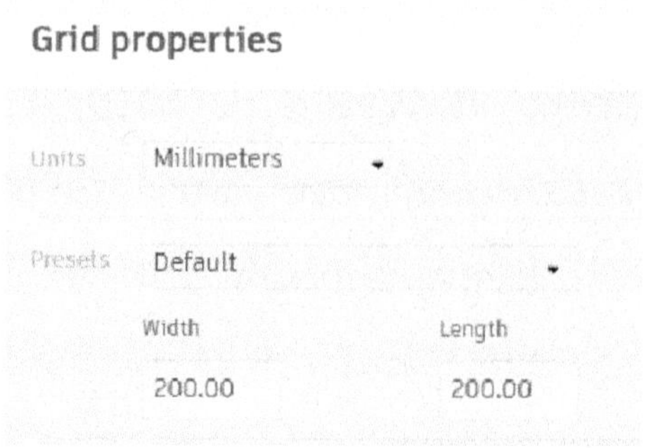

Grid properties

Units Millimeters

Presets Default

Width 200.00

Length 200.00

A plane has a grid on it to facilitate measurement visually (exactly like the grid for kids to learn writing letters). The plane that comes with all 3D software has grid by default, and you can easily customize the grid size to suit your unique need.

XYZ are axes. Every shape's position is default to X=0, Y=0, Z=0. X-axis is red, Y-axis is green, and Z-axis is blue.

In this example we have a cylinder created

on the workplane.

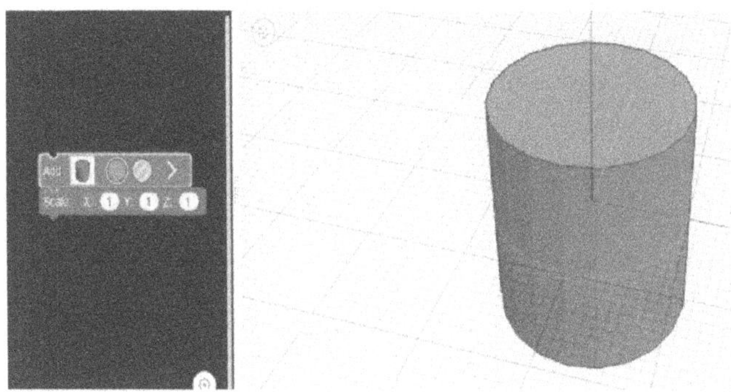

Now if we scale the X of this cylinder to a doubled value, the shape becomes like this (a side to side scaling):

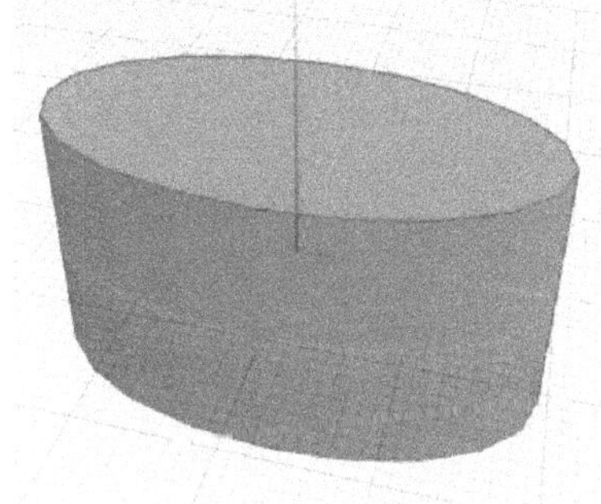

If we scale the Y of this cylinder to a doubled value, the shape becomes like this (a front to back scaling):

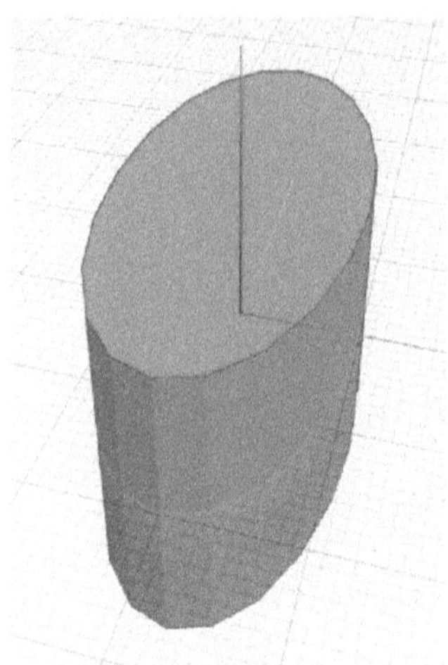

If we scale the Z of this cylinder to a doubled value, the shape becomes like this (a vertical scaling):

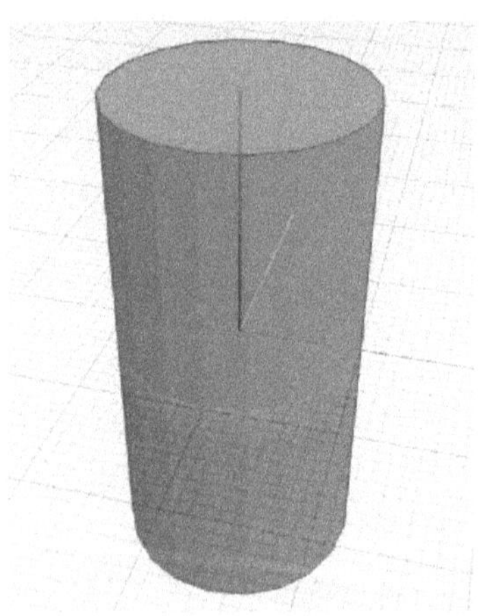

A point in a 3d space must have all 3 values

presented. Movement and rotation also work relying on the XYZ axis values.

This is rotation around the X axis:

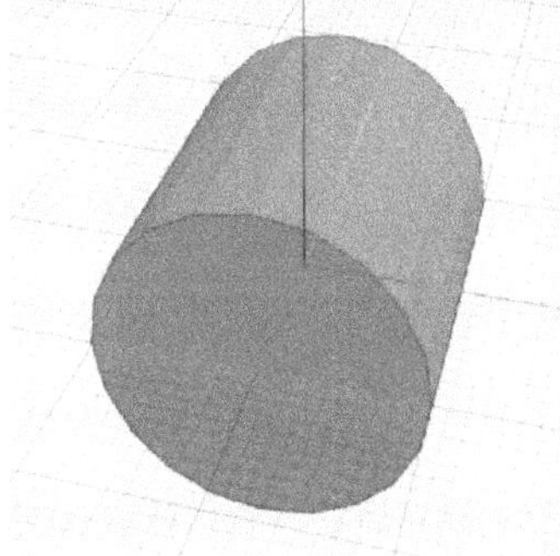

This is rotation around the Y axis:

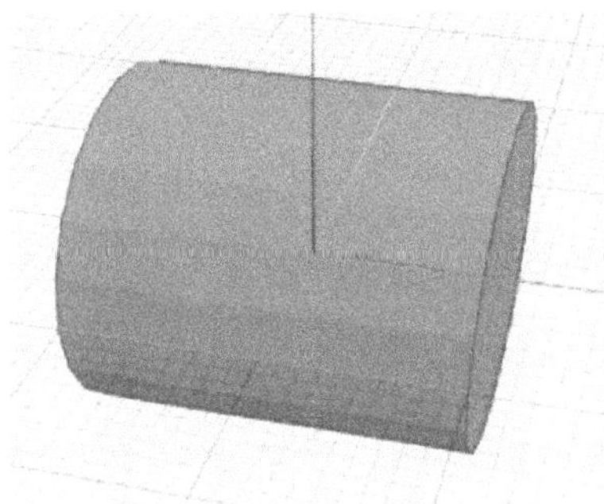

This is rotation around the Z axis, looks like nothing has happened as it is just like spinning while standing :):

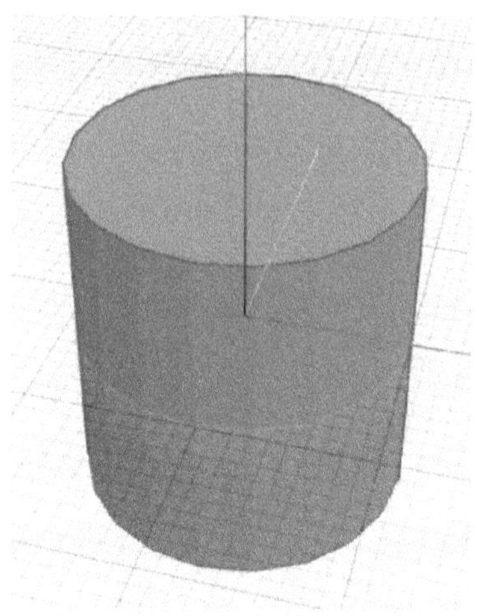

Sizing (aka scaling) works similarly although sometimes the axis can be confusing.

This is scaling along X:

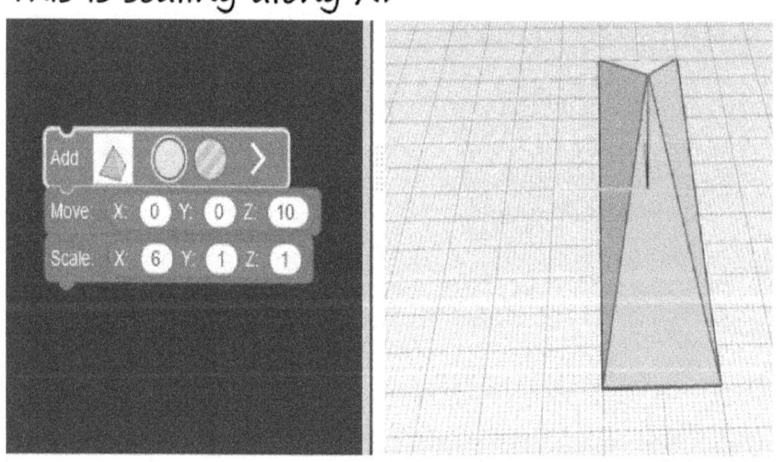

This is scaling along Y:

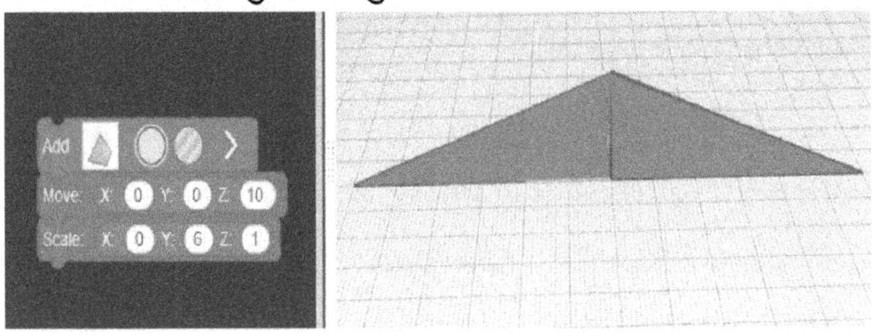

This is scaling along Z:

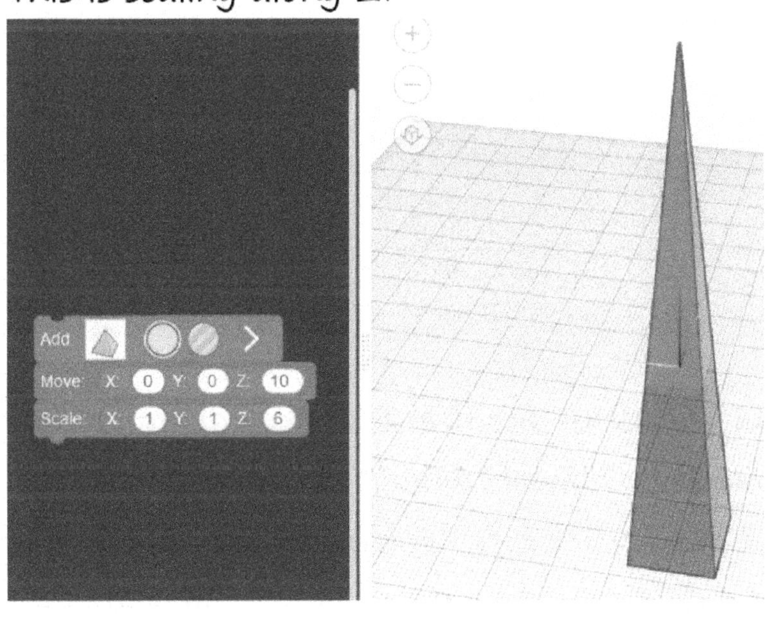

Tinkercad allows you to set the view (that is, how you look at the work plane and the objects on it). Some software describe it as

"Camera", while some use the term "perspective view".

Normally you start with a view in between TOP and FRONT. You can use the mouse to freely rotate the view, or click directly on the view icon to change view.

As previous mentioned, the default view mode is almost always a perspective one. Under such view, 3d objects are shown just like what can be seen photographically, that the object displays are scaled different based on distance with you.

Tinkercad does offer a flat view. This is a view primarily for technical drawing. It uses so called orthographic projection - that is, the object displays are NOT scaled different based on distance with you. They do not look photographically at all even though technically they are not 2D.

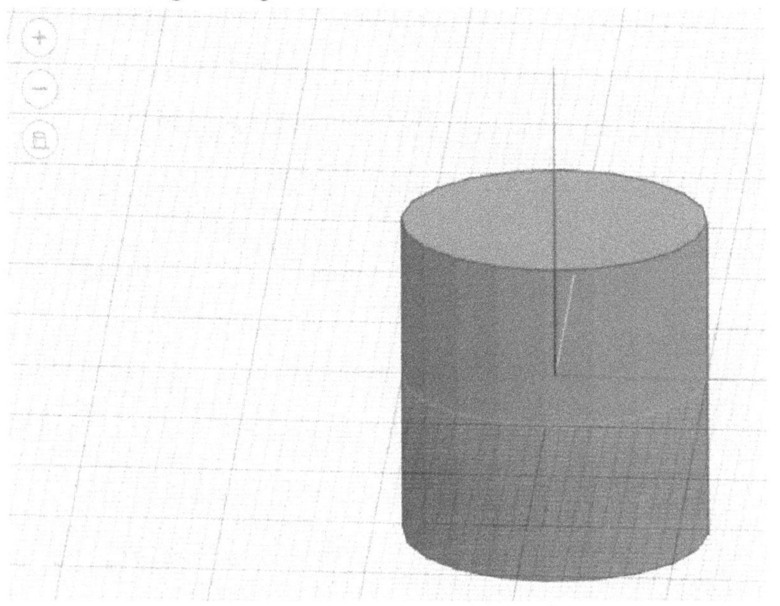

With zoom in, the canvas contents will appear larger. With zoom out, the canvas contents will appear smaller. They do not change the size of the 3d objects. They simply change the view size.

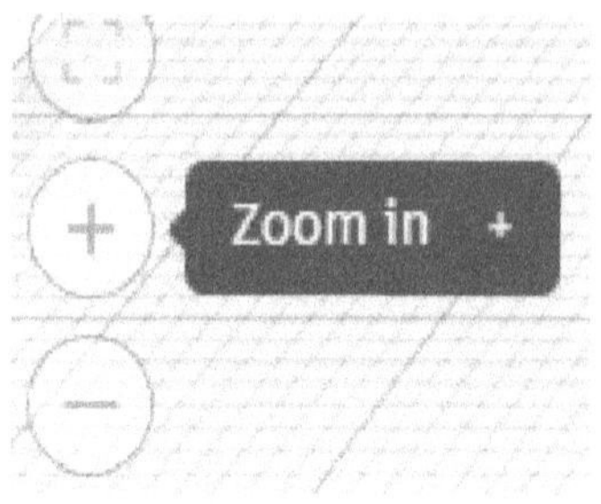

A solid is an object (often pre-made) with 3 dimensions, which are width, depth and height. It can come in different shapes.

Every 3d software provides you with some basic solid shapes (a.k.a primitives) to use. So is Tinkercad. In fact Tinkercad has a lot for you to choose from - they are like lego bricks that can be used as building blocks of a more complicated model.

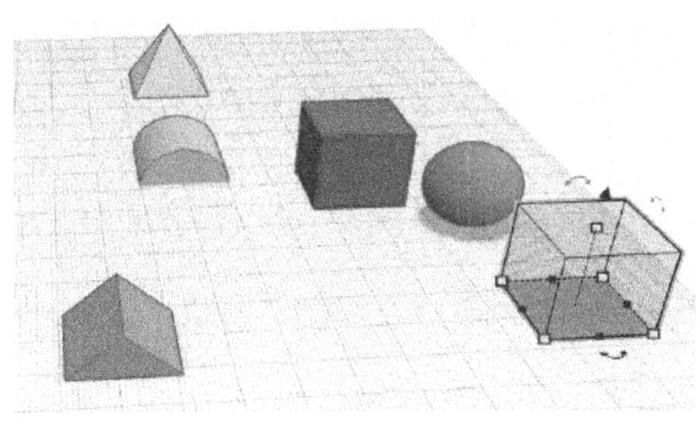

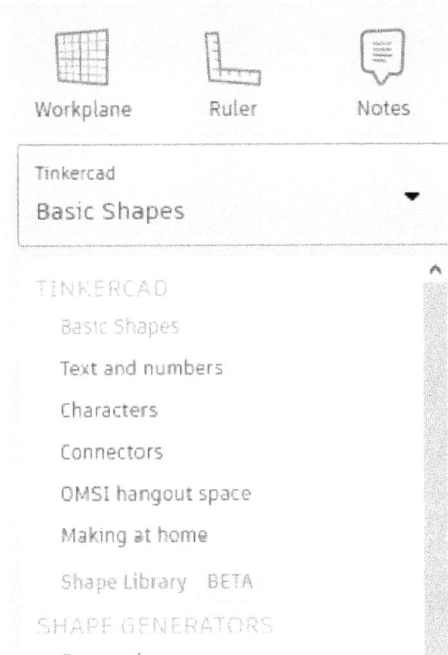

A 2d shape, in contrast, has only 2 dimensions, with either depth or height missing.

Traditional 3D modelling VS codeblocks

Traditional modelling is all about drag and drop. You use your mouse to do drag drop and all kinds of manipulation on the workplane.

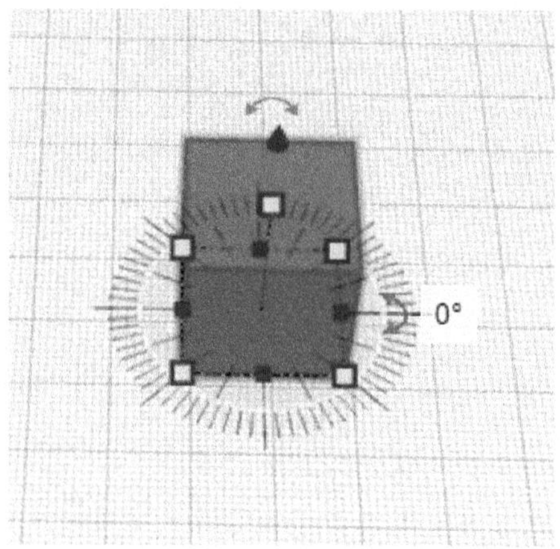

This way of modelling is easy in a sense. However, it is difficult to track and amend what have been done since the details are sort of "missing". And this is why we want to use code block programming to do the modelling instead.

Traditional programming is a text-based process which is also known as coding since you need to write text based code. This can be complicated and uneasy to learn.

Block-based programming uses modular graphical blocks to represent instruction code so that they are easier to understand and "write". In Tinkercad Codeblock, even shapes are made available as blocks.

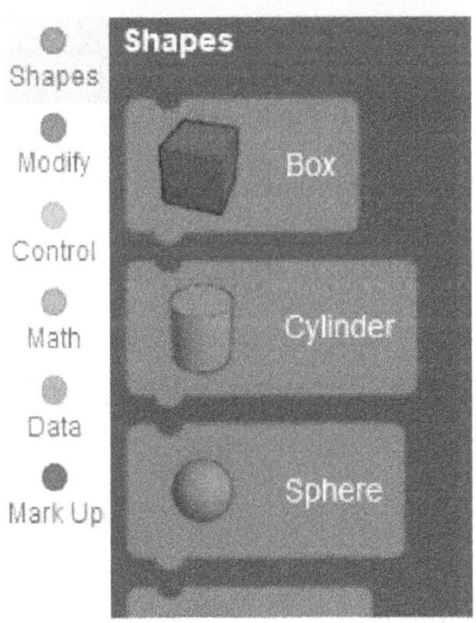

When you drag a block into the workplane, you can specify the details such as size and color. Because these values can be modified whenever necessary even after many steps, you can exercise complete tracking and control over it.

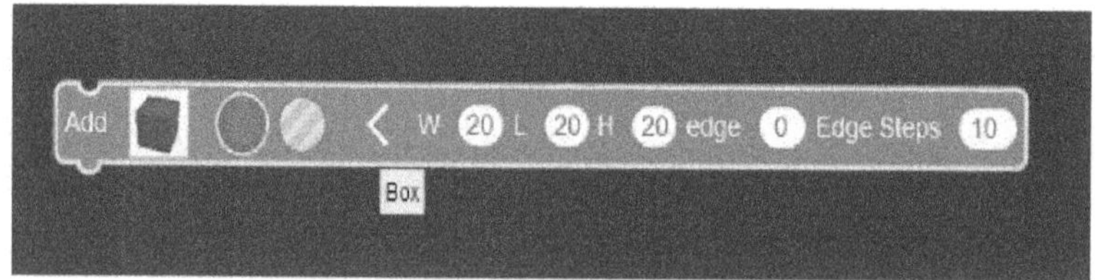

All subsequent modifications can be done (and undone) through code block and can be fine tuned easily. In the example below, the shape after creation is rotated and scaled.

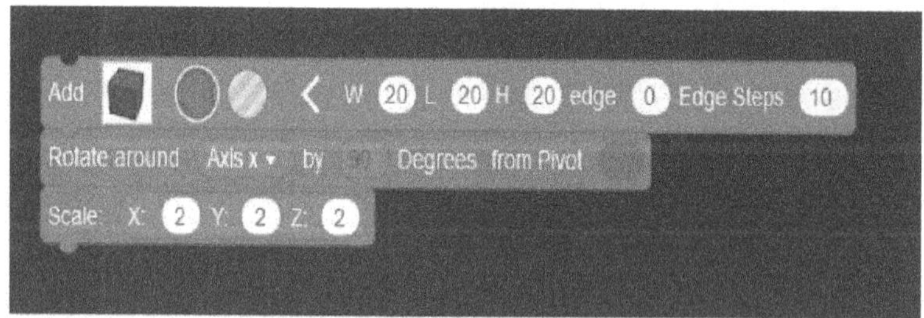

For these to take effect, you need to hit the play button.

Or you can "play" the code one block at a time via:

In a sense, this code block process works like "scripting" - it allows you to script the entire 3D modelling process.

Whenever adjustments or changes are needed, you modify the script and replay it to create the models. This is NOT the same as programming.

In modern programming, things are structured to respond to events, that the code reacts to predefined events that can happen anytime out of order.

In scripting, there is a top down order of things. The code blocks are executed line by line one by one based on the order you arrange for them.

Another question people always come up with is whether or not all code blocks must be put "together" as one block, like this one:

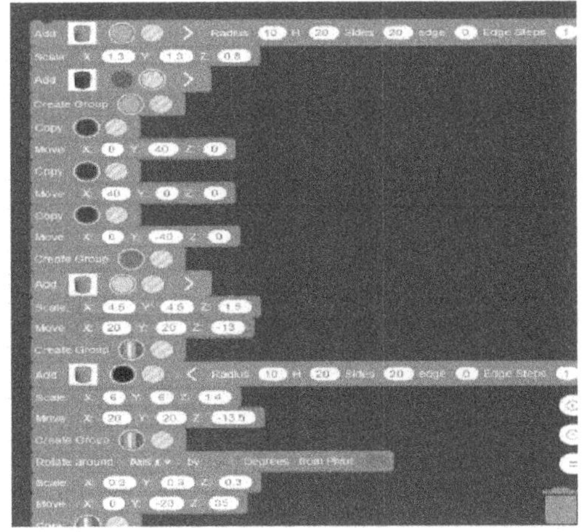

The answer is NO. See this, the add blocks are not really "together" but the end result is identical.

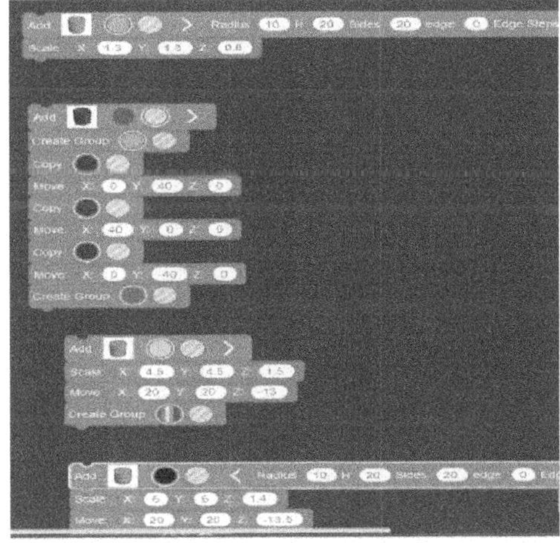

The order of execution is important but as long as the code blocks are arrange in a top down manner then it will be alright.

To remind yourself what you have written, you can always use the Comment block to add comments to your code:

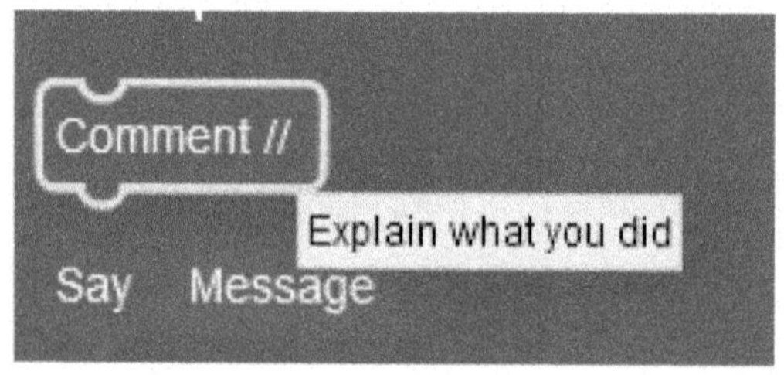

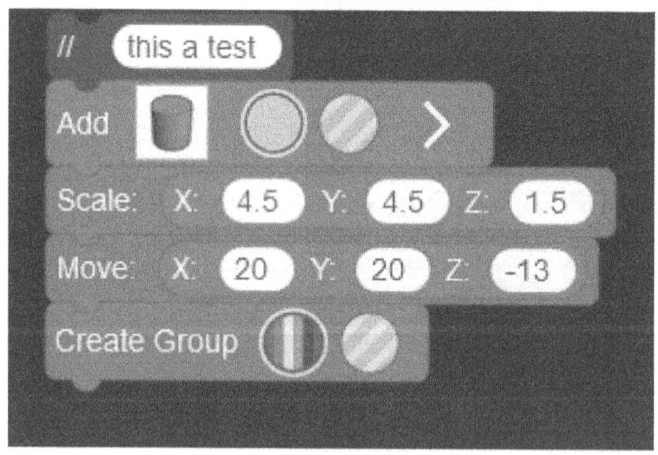

The 3d models that have been created can be exported and be saved in your local computer drive. There are different format available. If your goal is to make 3d prints, choose STL.

Do note that you cannot export the code blocks. You can only export the model created with the code blocks. If you choose the STL format, the 3D Viewer can comes with Windows 10 can open the file for viewing.

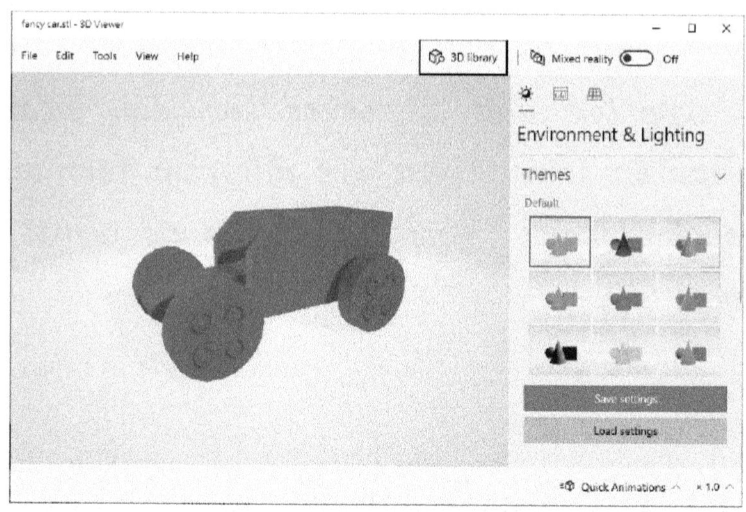

This book focuses on the basics that can get you started quickly.

Project 1 - A basic car

A simple basic car has 5 main parts, which are the car body and 4 wheels. Some initial planning may be helpful. How large is the car going to be? Color? How large should be the wheels be? Are all wheels of the same size?

The car body should have a blue color.

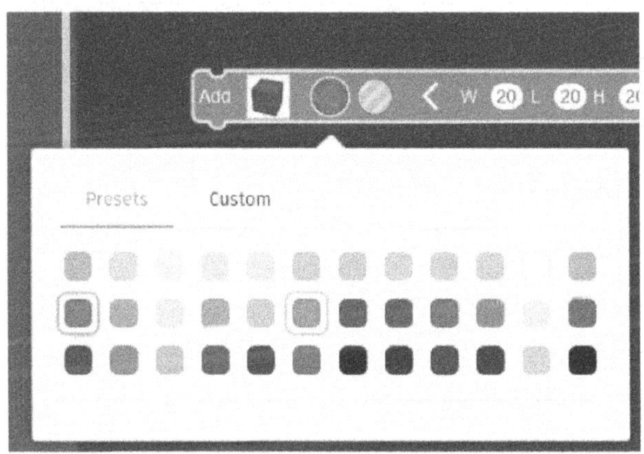

It should be of a rectangular type, meaning we have to adjust the width:

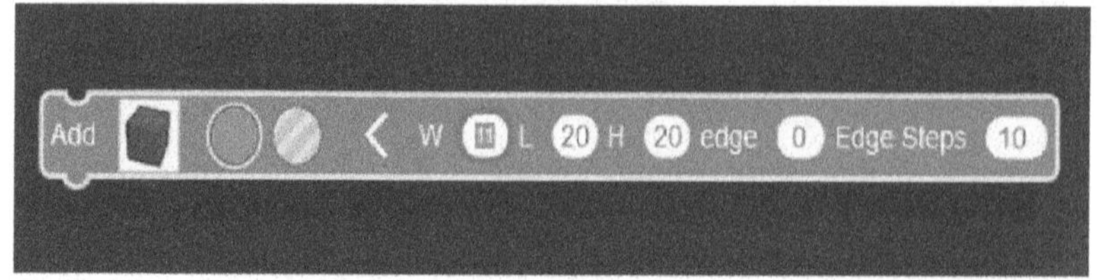

We want to move the shape up so it can stay on top of the work plane. So we add a move block with a change in the Z value.

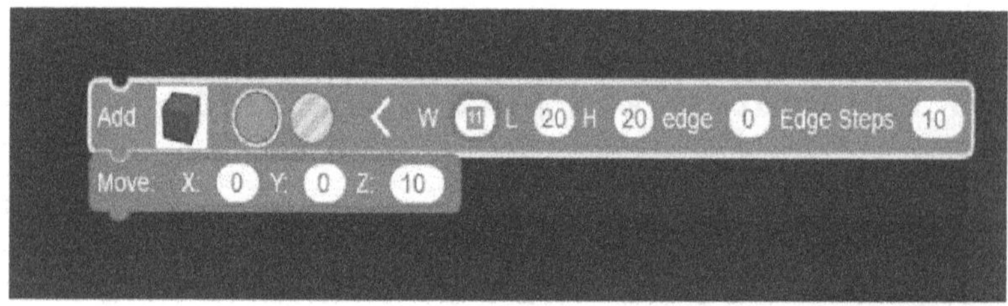

This is what we have so far:

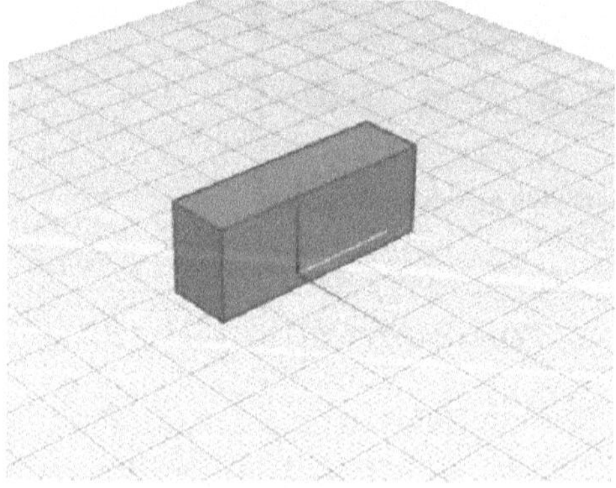

For wheels we need to use the Tube shape. Change the color to black.

Except for the radius which dictates the wheel size, the other values can be left unchanged since we can always change them later. The default radius is 10 and we may change it to, say, 6.

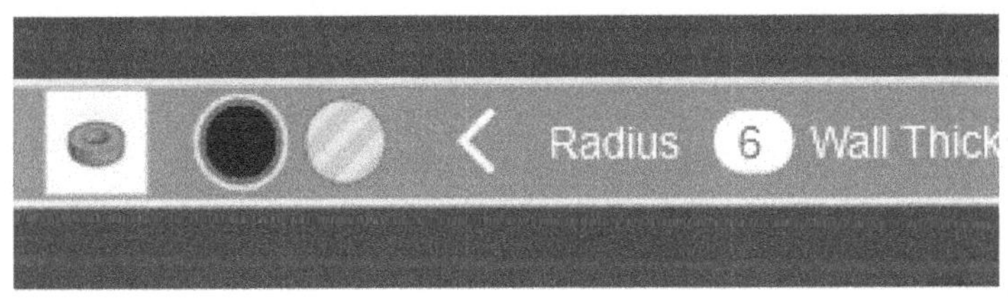

Then we need to properly position it. By default it lays flat on the workplane.

We need to use a rotate block to rotate the wheel by 90 degrees along the Y axis.

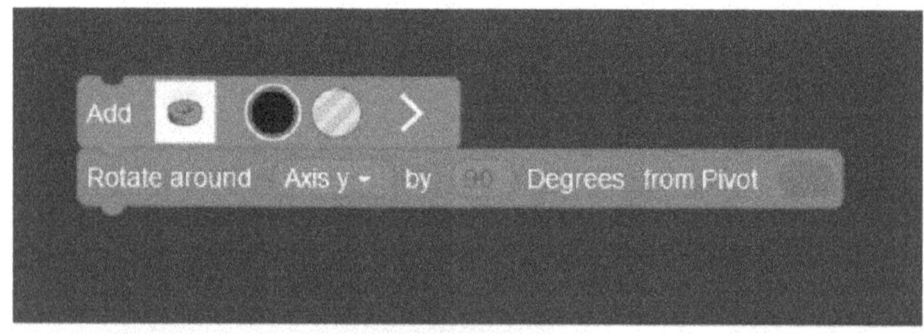

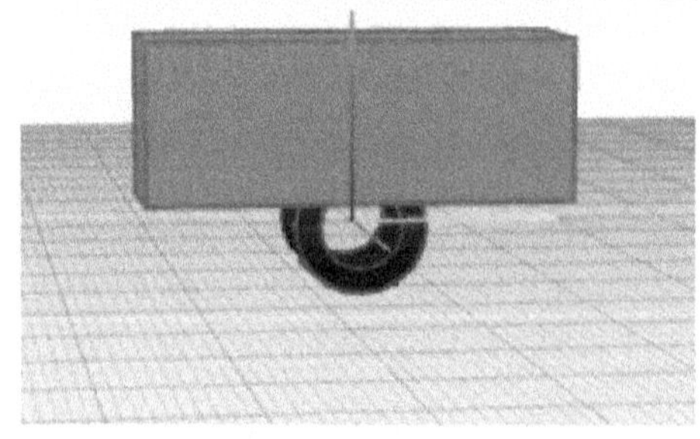

Then we need to move it to the proper position.

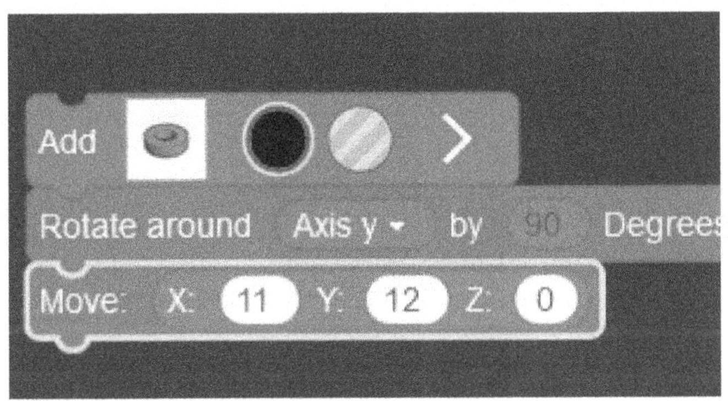

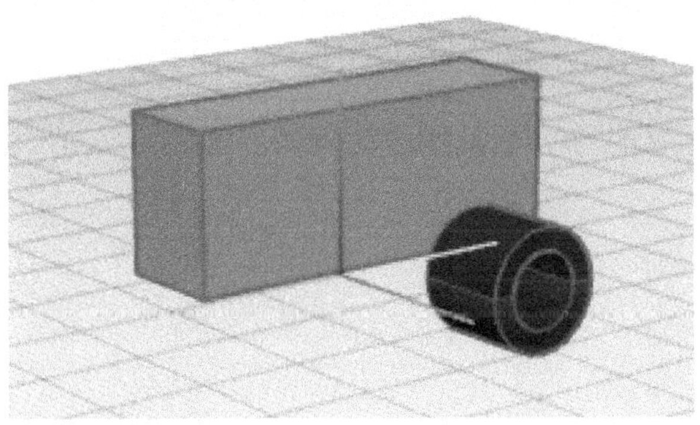

Now we need to make copies of this wheel. To allow for easy identification, we use a different color for the front wheels.

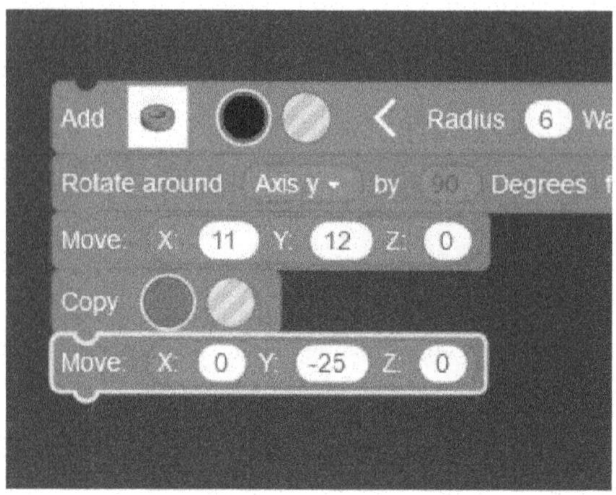

You want to know that the calculation of the XYZ position is based on the last known position, NOT based on the day one position. In other words, the last known position becomes 0,0,0 for the next one.

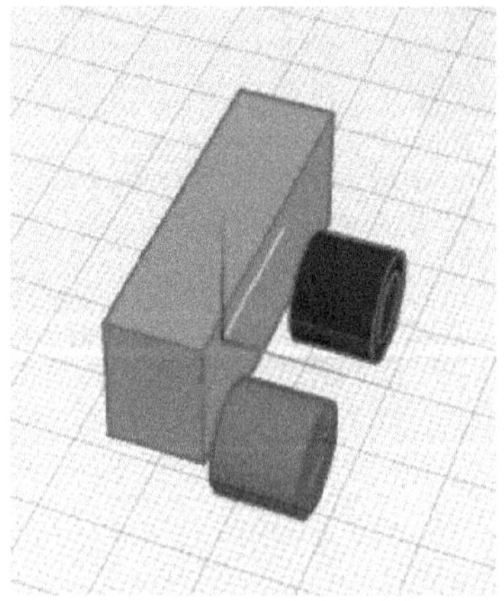

You can right click on a copy block and choose Duplicate to copy the block:

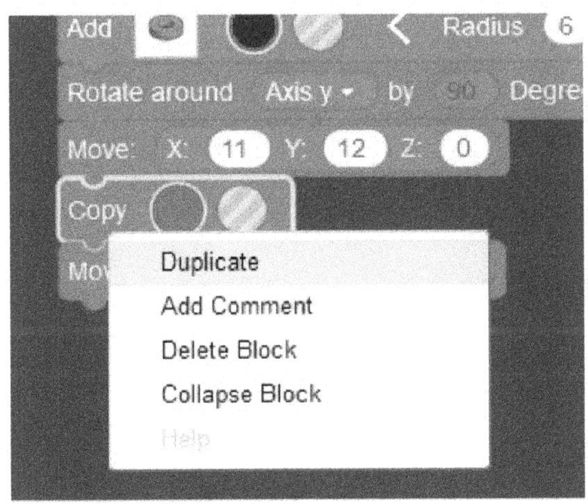

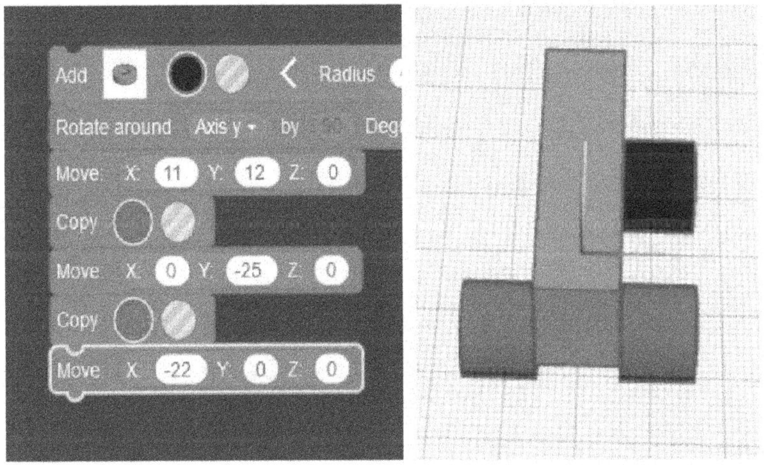

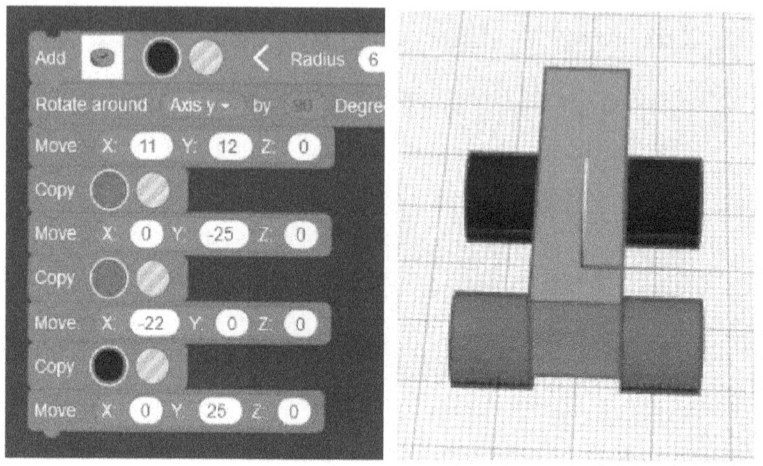

Now we have a "car" built with multiple individual parts. In order to be able to manipulate the car as one single object, we should group all the parts together. So we select all of them and create one group that includes all of them.

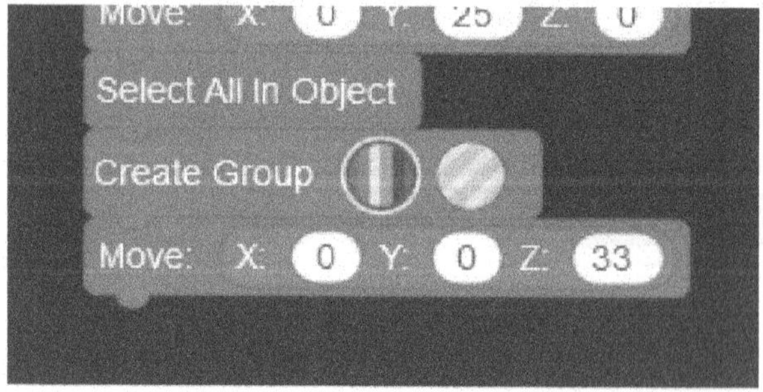

Now we can move or rotate or scale the entire car as one entity.

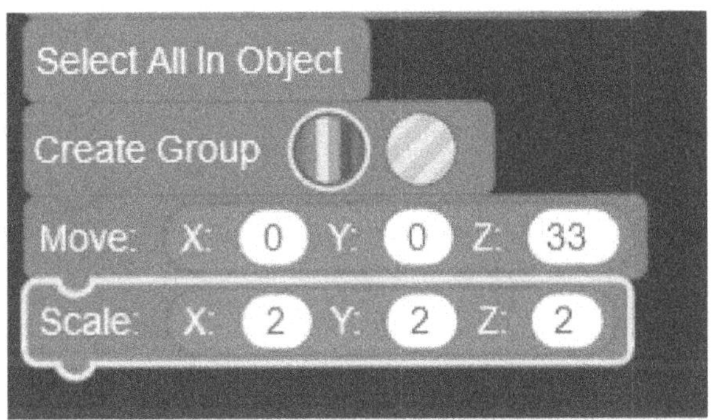

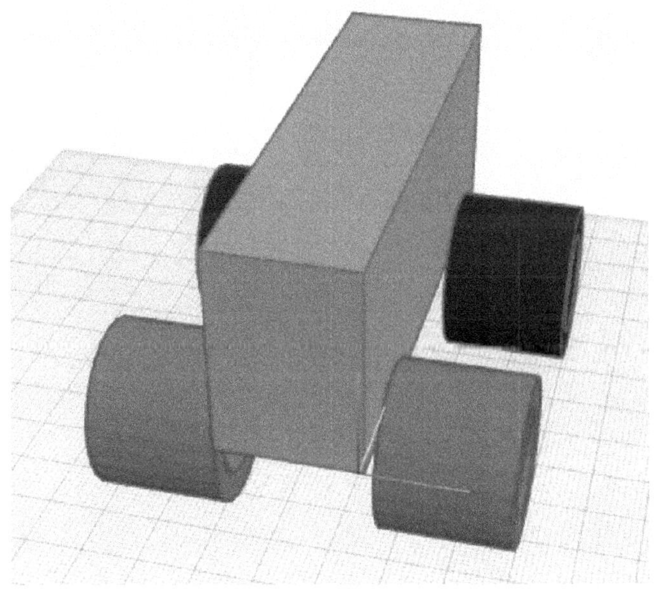

Note that there is no need to explicitly save

anything. Everything stays with your browser and the cloud. Whenever you choose to create a new design, the existing one is automatically "saved" so you can work on it again next time.

Project 2 - A car with fancy features

Now we want to add a spoiler to the rear end of the car. We use the Wedge shape for it. We also need to rotate and scale it properly to make it looks like a spoiler.

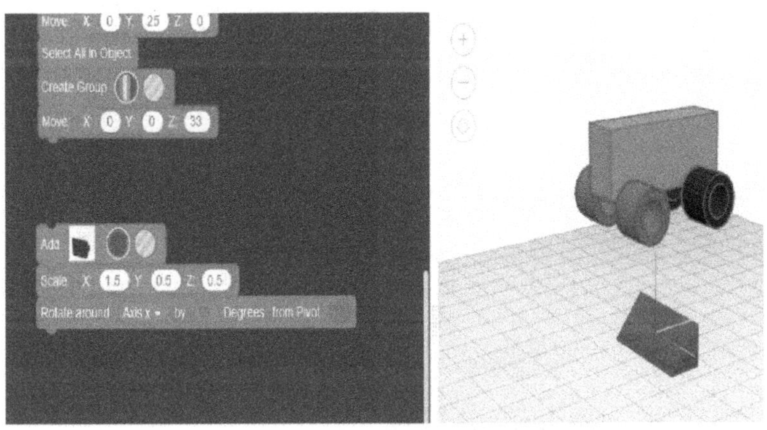

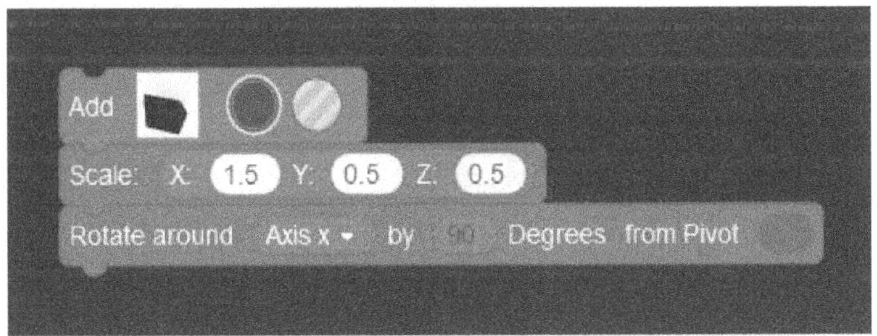

Finally you need to move it up so it stays

correctly at the rear end of the car body. Note that scaling can be set using different values along different axis. In this case we want to widen the spoiler so we scale along X with a larger value.

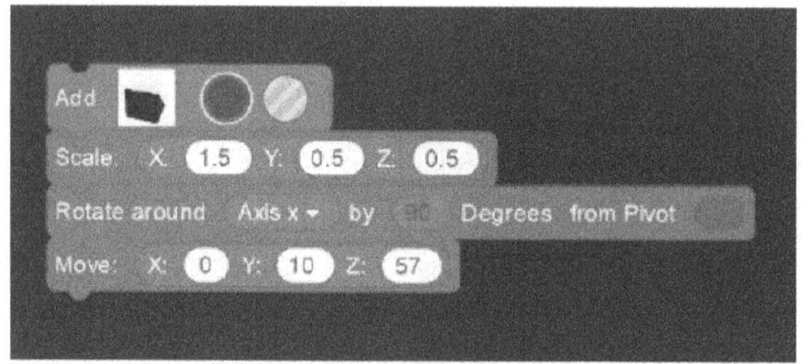

After the spoiler, we need to give the car an exhaust pipe. We can use a tube, then resize and rotate it properly. The values have to be adjusted carefully.

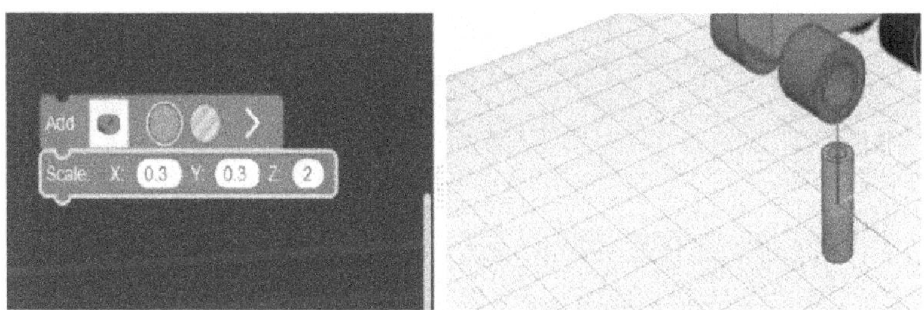

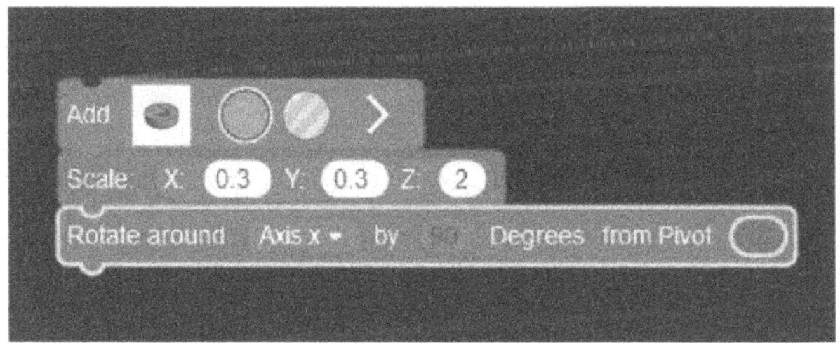

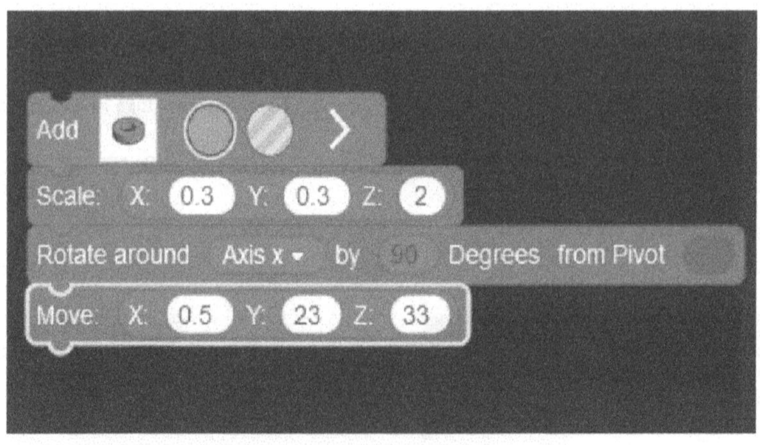

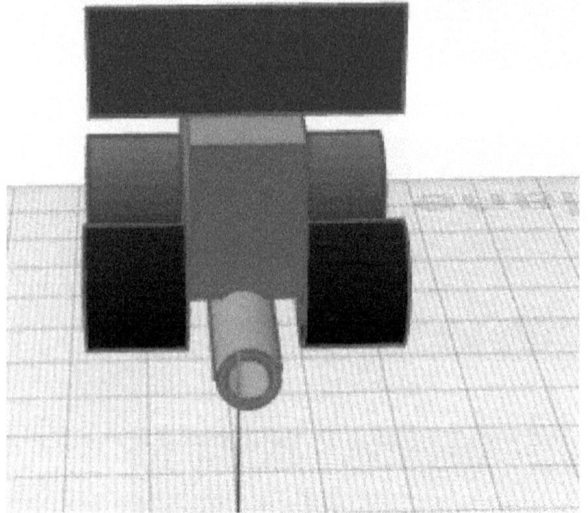

Once they are all in place, it is time to make final adjustment to the size and position values before grouping them together again.

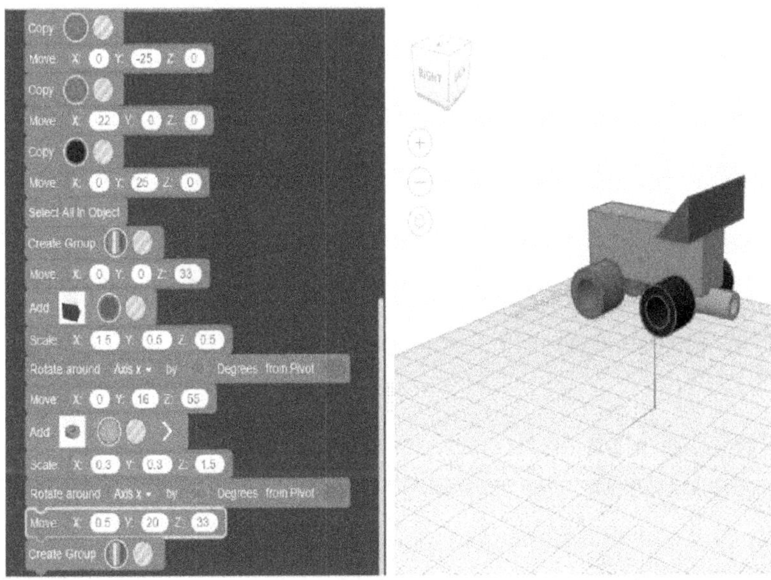
Copy
Move X: 0 Y: -25 Z: 0
Copy
Move X: -22 Y: 0 Z: 0
Copy
Move X: 0 Y: 25 Z: 0
Select All in Object
Create Group
Move X: 0 Y: 0 Z: 33
Add
Scale X: 1.5 Y: 0.5 Z: 0.5
Rotate around Axis x by Degrees from Pivot
Move X: 0 Y: 16 Z: 55
Add
Scale X: 0.3 Y: 0.3 Z: 1.5
Rotate around Axis x by Degrees from Pivot
Move X: 0.5 Y: 20 Z: 33
Create Group

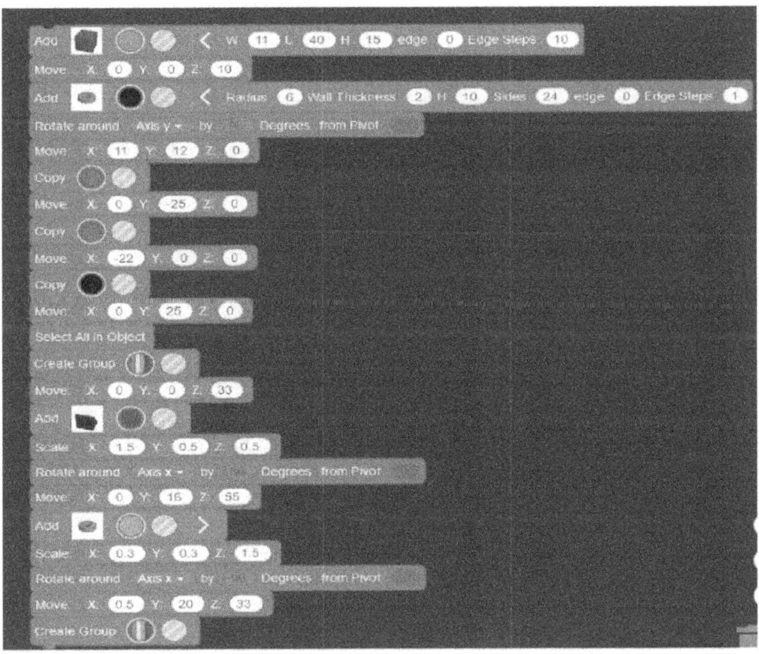
Add W 11 L 40 H 15 edge 0 Edge Steps 10
Move X: 0 Y: 0 Z: 10
Add Radius 6 Wall Thickness 2 H 10 Sides 24 edge 0 Edge Steps 1
Rotate around Axis y by Degrees from Pivot
Move X: 11 Y: 12 Z: 0
Copy
Move X: 0 Y: -25 Z: 0
Copy
Move X: -22 Y: 0 Z: 0
Copy
Move X: 0 Y: 25 Z: 0
Select All in Object
Create Group
Move X: 0 Y: 0 Z: 33
Add
Scale X: 1.5 Y: 0.5 Z: 0.5
Rotate around Axis x by Degrees from Pivot
Move X: 0 Y: 16 Z: 55
Add
Scale X: 0.3 Y: 0.3 Z: 1.5
Rotate around Axis x by Degrees from Pivot
Move X: 0.5 Y: 20 Z: 33
Create Group

Now you have all the blocks in one screen. You can make changes to the values, or add/delete code blocks as needed.

To delete a block, pull it out and drag to the trash bin:

To adjust the creation speed (that is, to play back the code blocks), manipulate this:

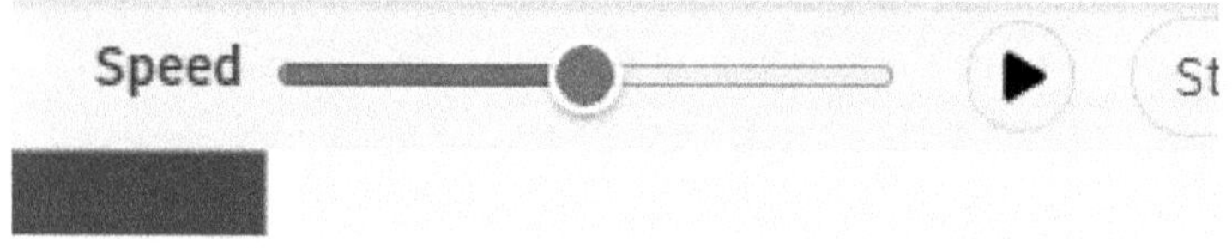

To see the effect step by step block by block, use this:

Project 3 - Tire rim

In this project we want to create a good looking tire rim for the wheels.

To make things work, you need to know the difference in the way you add a shape. As can be seen from the photo below, when you add a shape the default selection is a solid:

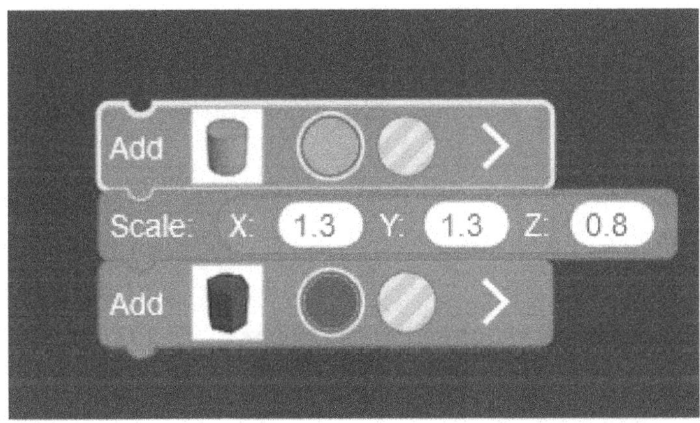

Default solid is on the left: 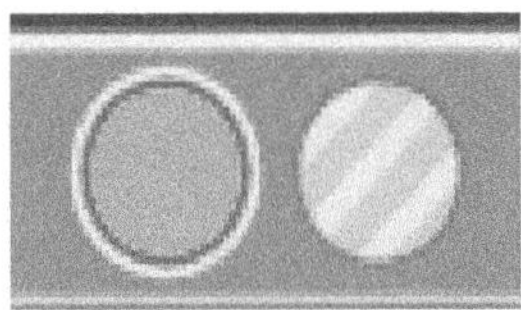

This is what is created (cylinder and polygon shapes combined):

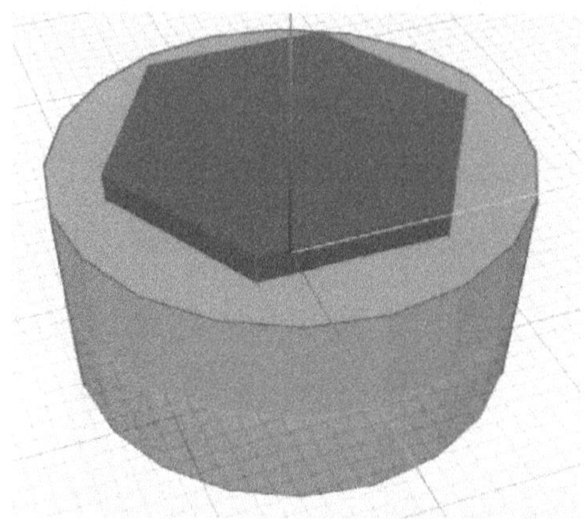

Now when we group them together under the boolean mode and pick a color for the group:

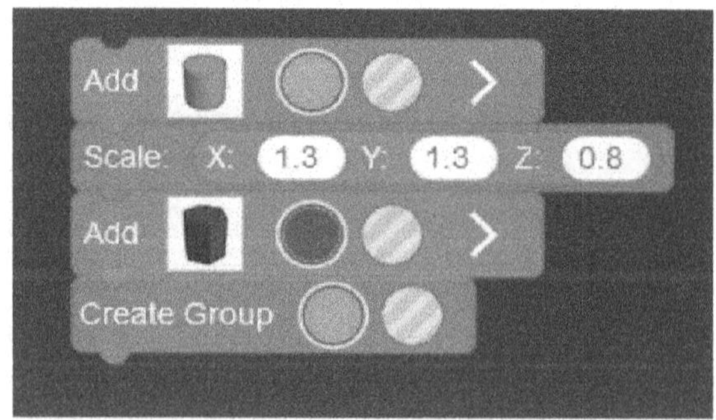

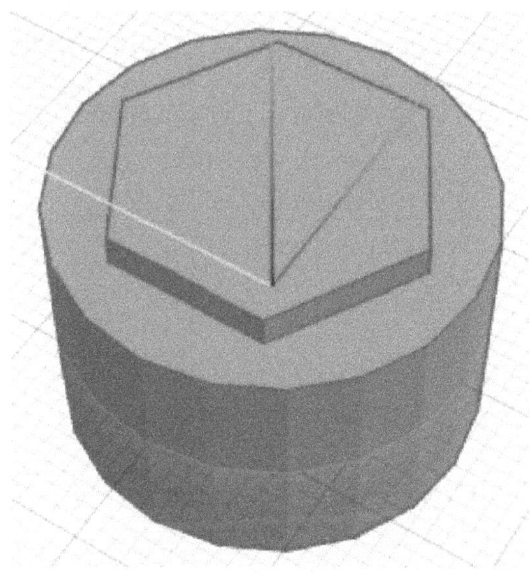

The resulting object is a combined one. In fact, geometry boolean is a special operation. See this:

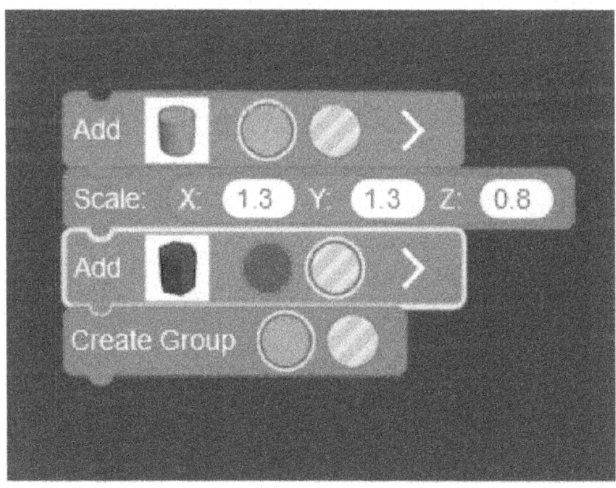

The second shape (the polygon) has been switched to the second mode (the mode on the right, sort of like an "empty" mode):

The result of grouping them is like a subtraction:

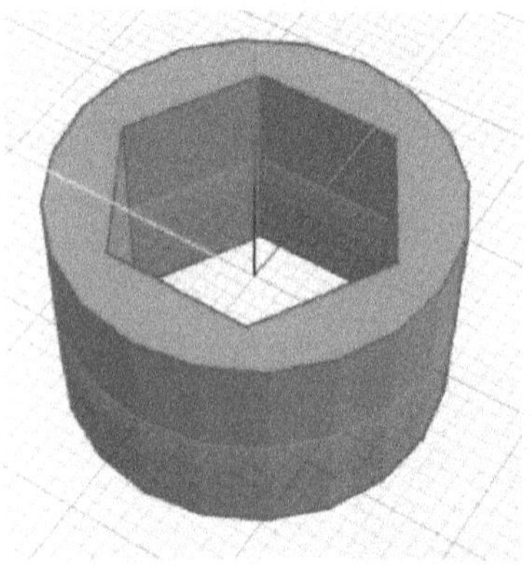

This is how you create special shape, through subtracting (cutting that is). Now lets create 3 more copies out of it. We need to use 3 sets of copy block. To speed things up, right click and choose Duplicate:

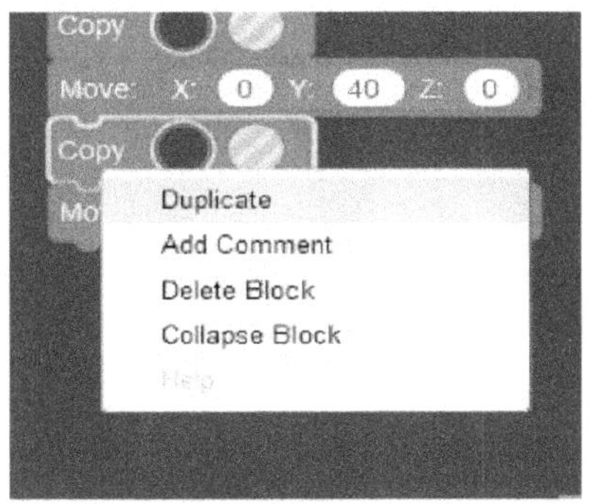

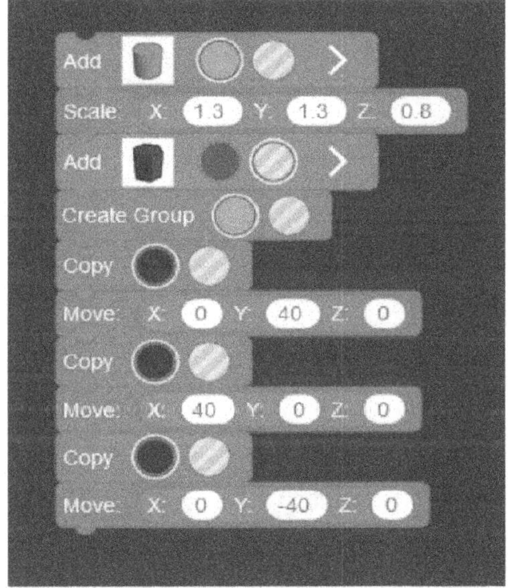

Note the axis values specified in the move blocks. They are arranged in a way that have the shapes laid out like this:

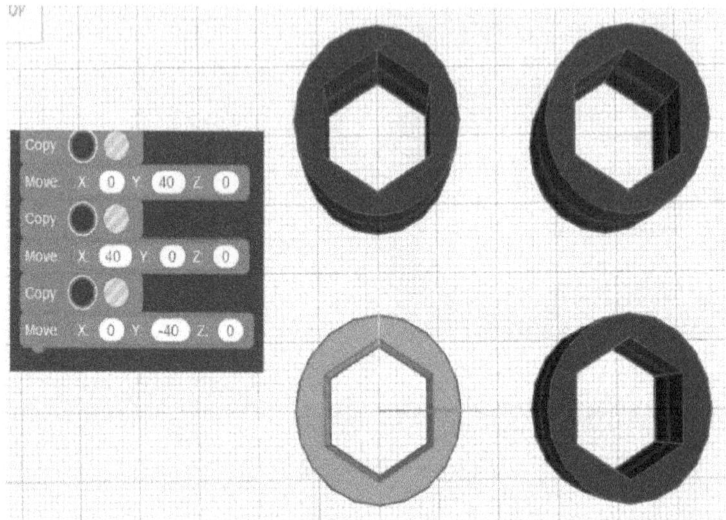

Now we should create a group for them (and give them the same color) so they can be moved and rotated together.

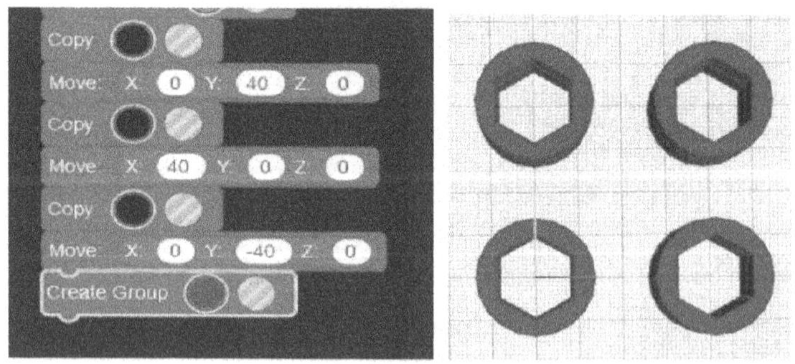

Now lets create the main frame for the rim, again using the cylinder shape, then scale and position it accordingly..

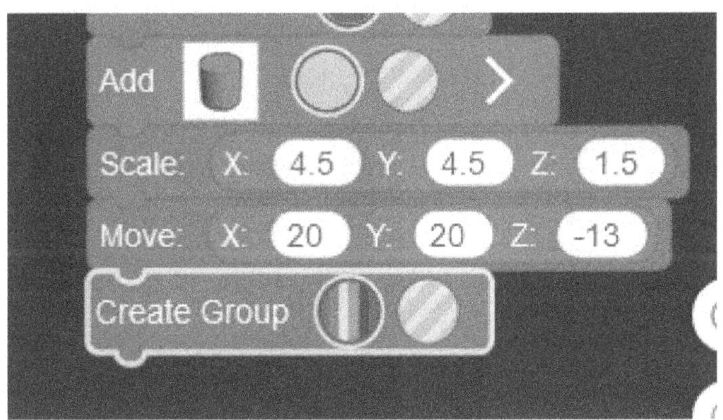

Finally we group all of them together to produce a nice looking tire rim:

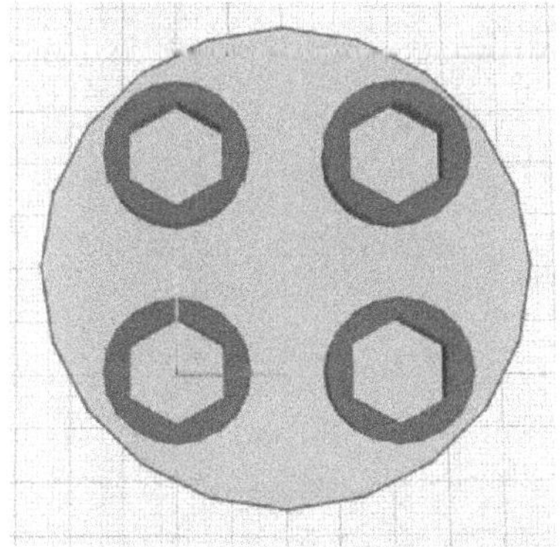

Now we need to create a tire to wrap around the rim. It is simply a larger cylinder.

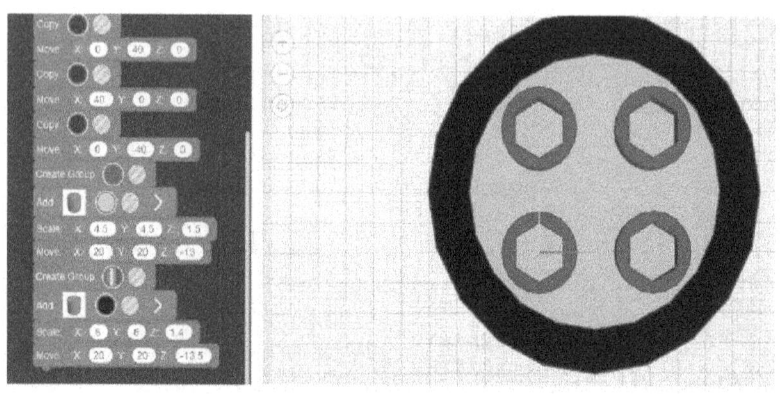

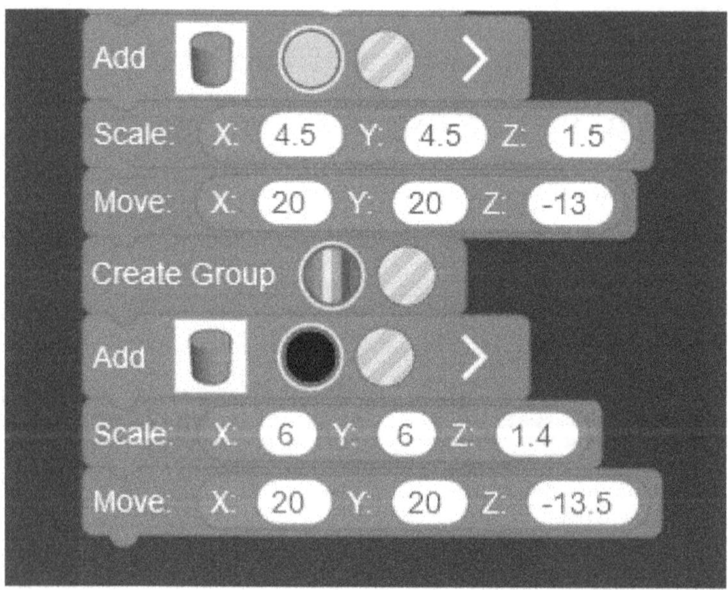

Just for fun: we can give this wheel a rotating effect. Make sure everything is grouped into one, then pick the Repeat block under Control (this block allows you to repeat whatever is contained inside it for the number of time specified):

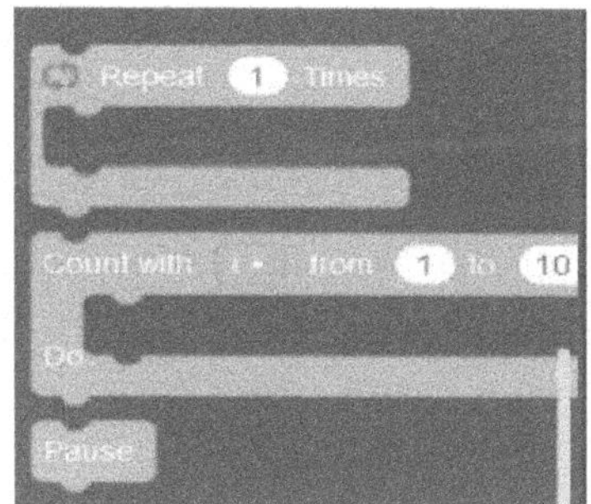

To allow the wheel to spin, use this block:

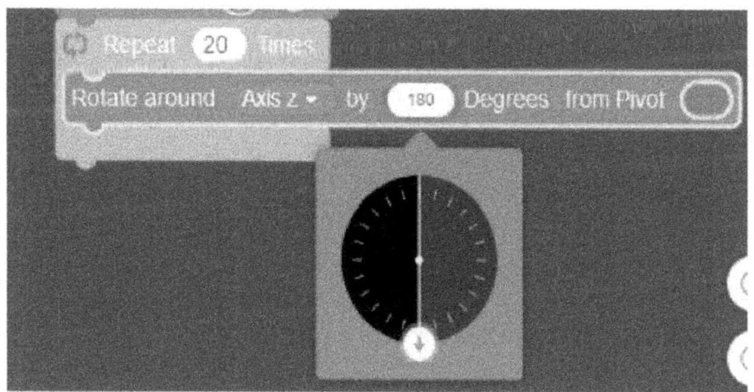

Now we want to properly size and position this wheel, then make 3 more copies out of it. The code blocks below position and size the wheel before making copies.

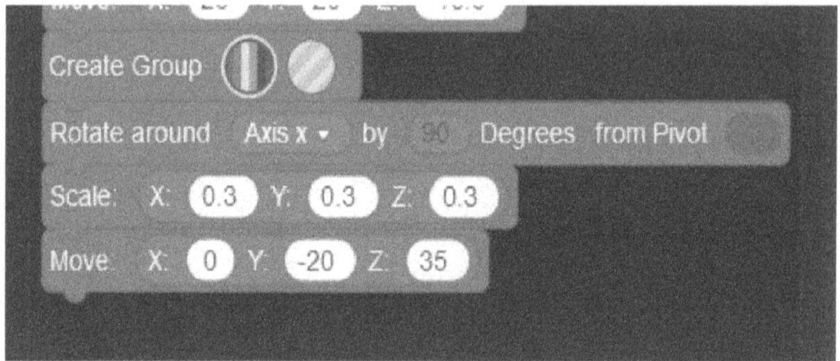

Now we make copies and arrange their locations.

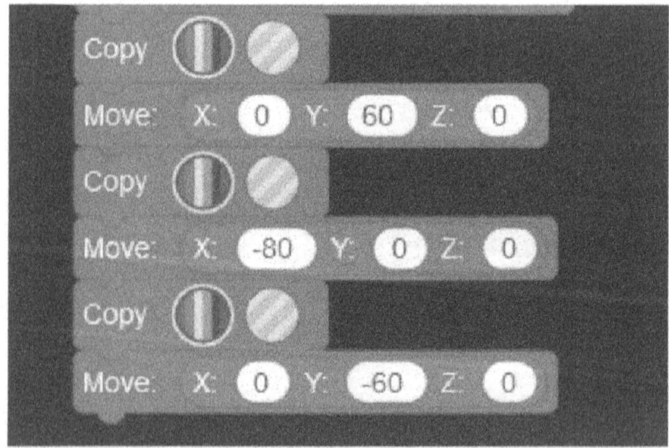

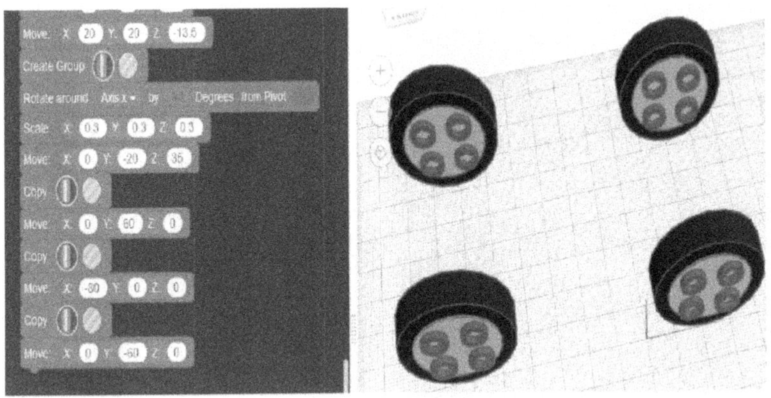

Note that two of the wheels need to be "flipped" so they are facing correctly. So we need to add two rotate blocks.

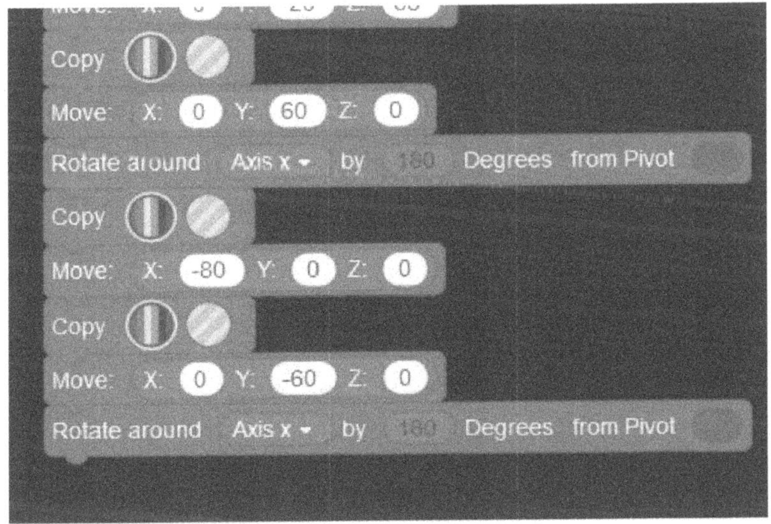

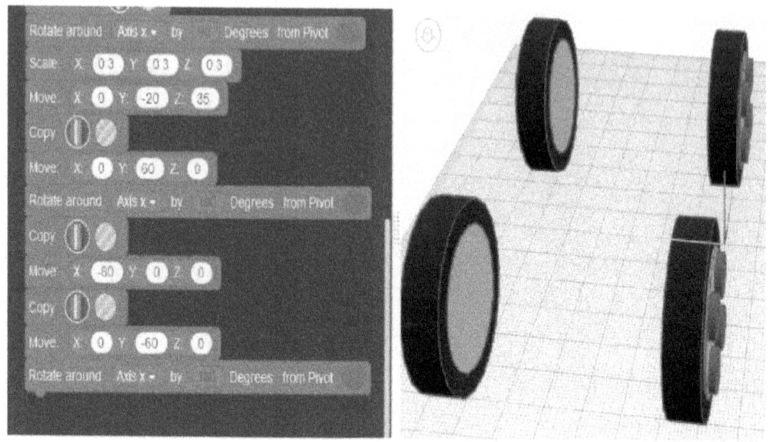

Now we want to add shafts to connect the wheels. Cylinders are fine for this purpose.

We need to create, size and position a shaft properly so it can connect two wheels. The size (in radius) and length (the H value) can be defined at the time of adding the shape.

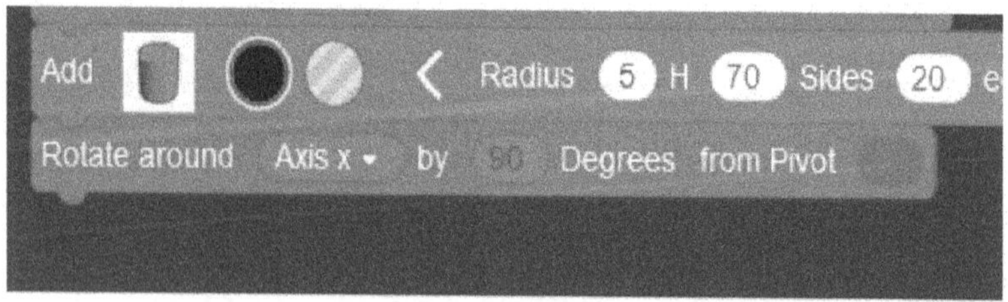

Positioning the shaft requires careful adjustment. Once the first shaft is properly in place we can make a copy out of it for another pair of wheels.

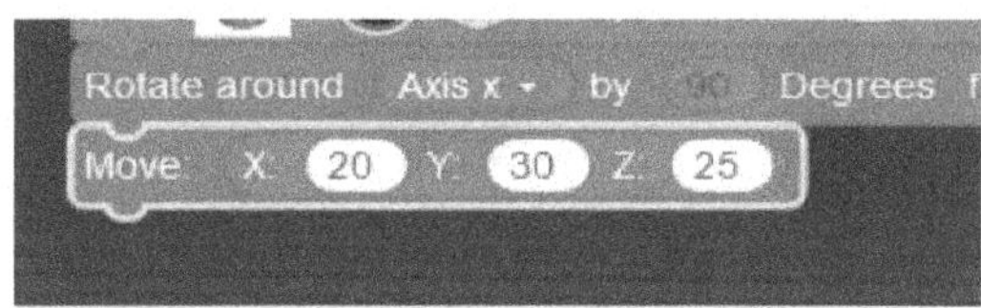

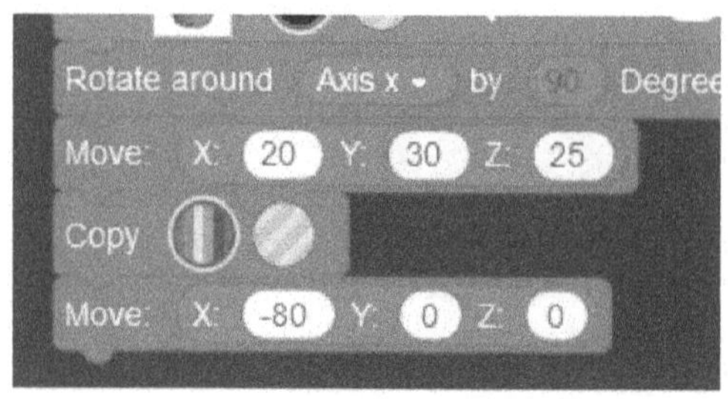

Now we need to have a center linkage that links the two shafts together. A long polygon can do the trick.

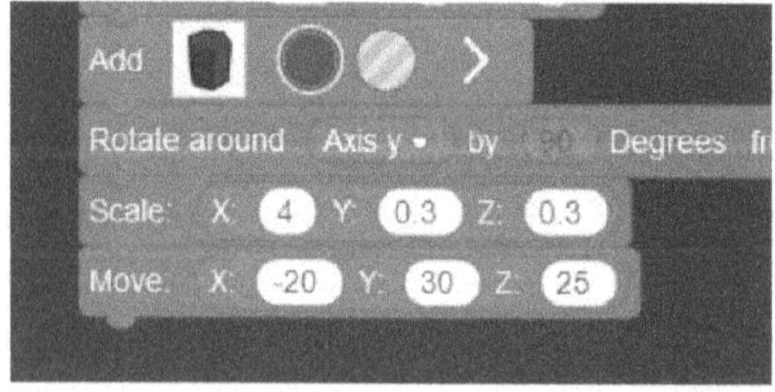

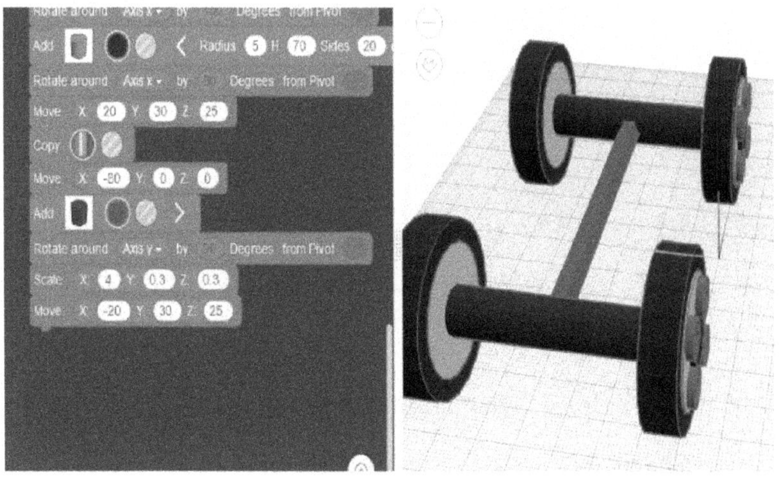

Finally, don;t forget to add a Create Group block to group everything together once again.

Project 4 - Car body

In this project we aim to create a better looking car body. It should be more than a simple rectangle. It should look more stylish.

We will use a box for the rectangular body and a round roof for the front bumper-like structure.

First we work on the body. We create a box with the proper size and move it.

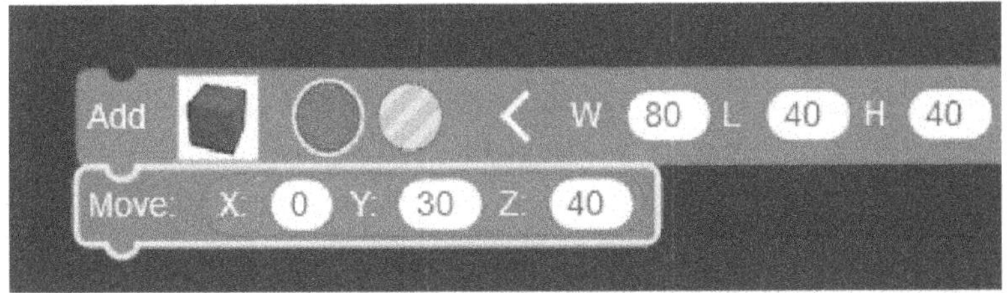

Now we want the body to have a "forehead" section. We will use a wedge shape to cut away part of the front section.

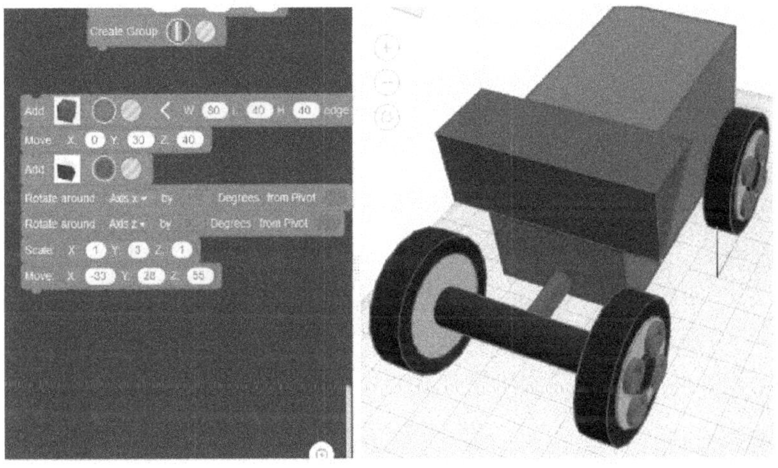

We rotate, size and position the wedge.

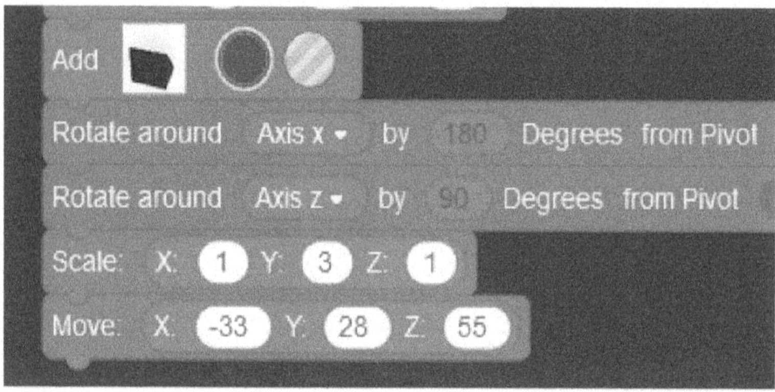

Then we change the mode of the wedge and create a group, effectively making a cut.

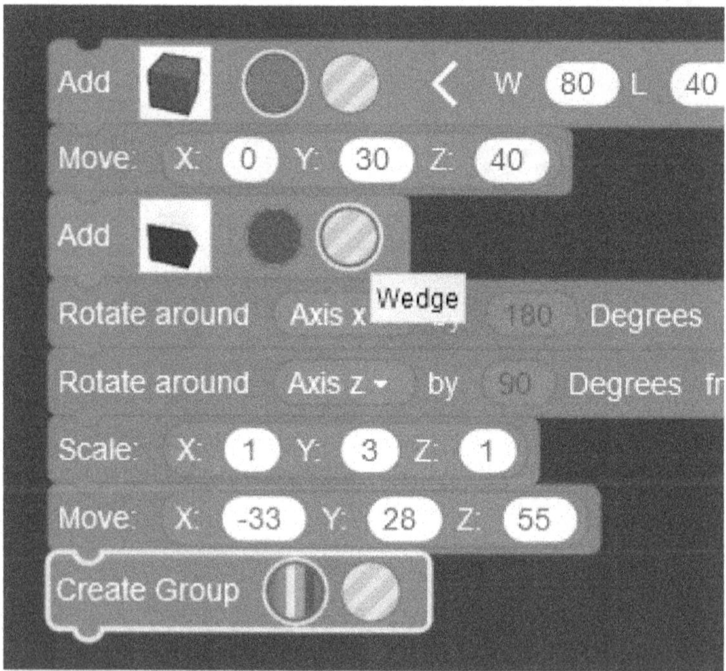

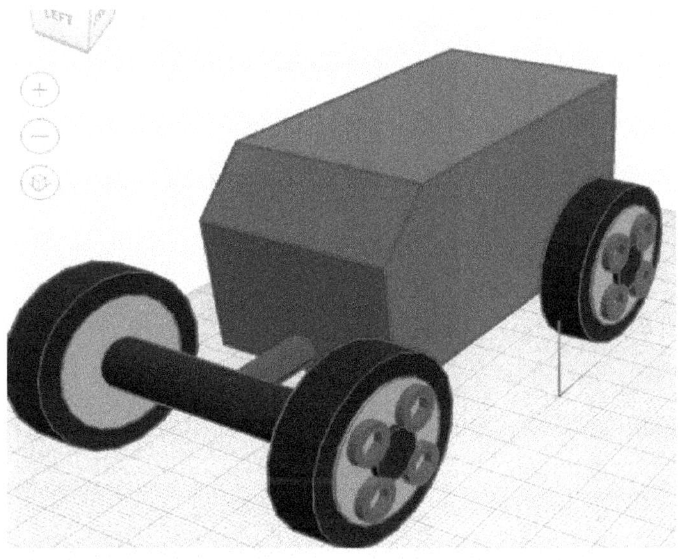

To create an empty compartment inside the box for the driver, we can actually make copies of the wedge and use them to cut the box as needed:

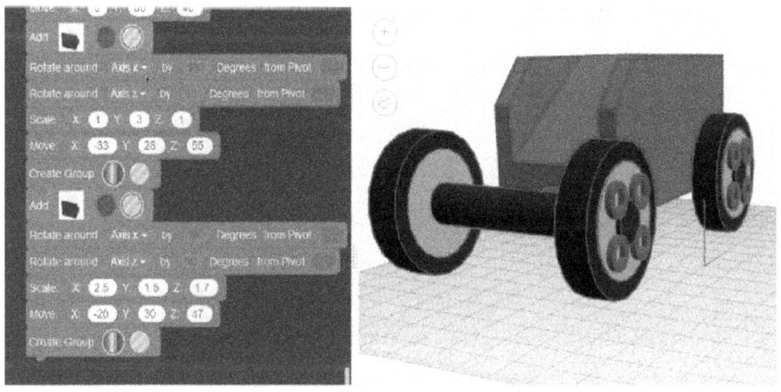

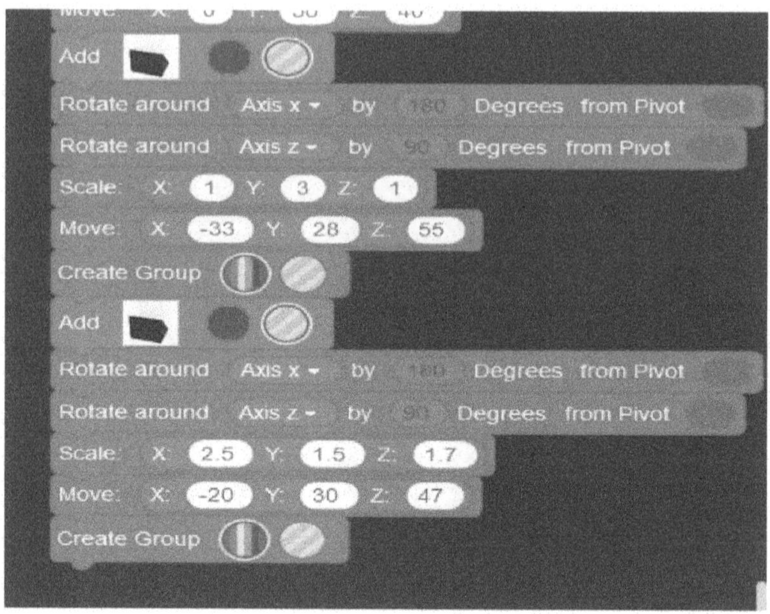

Now is the time to create the front structure using the round roof shape.

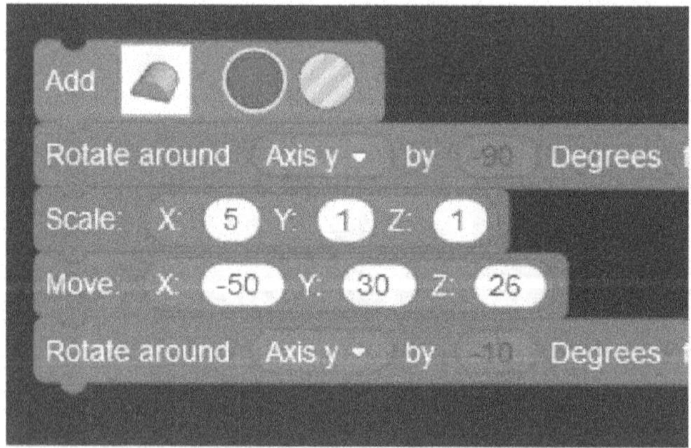

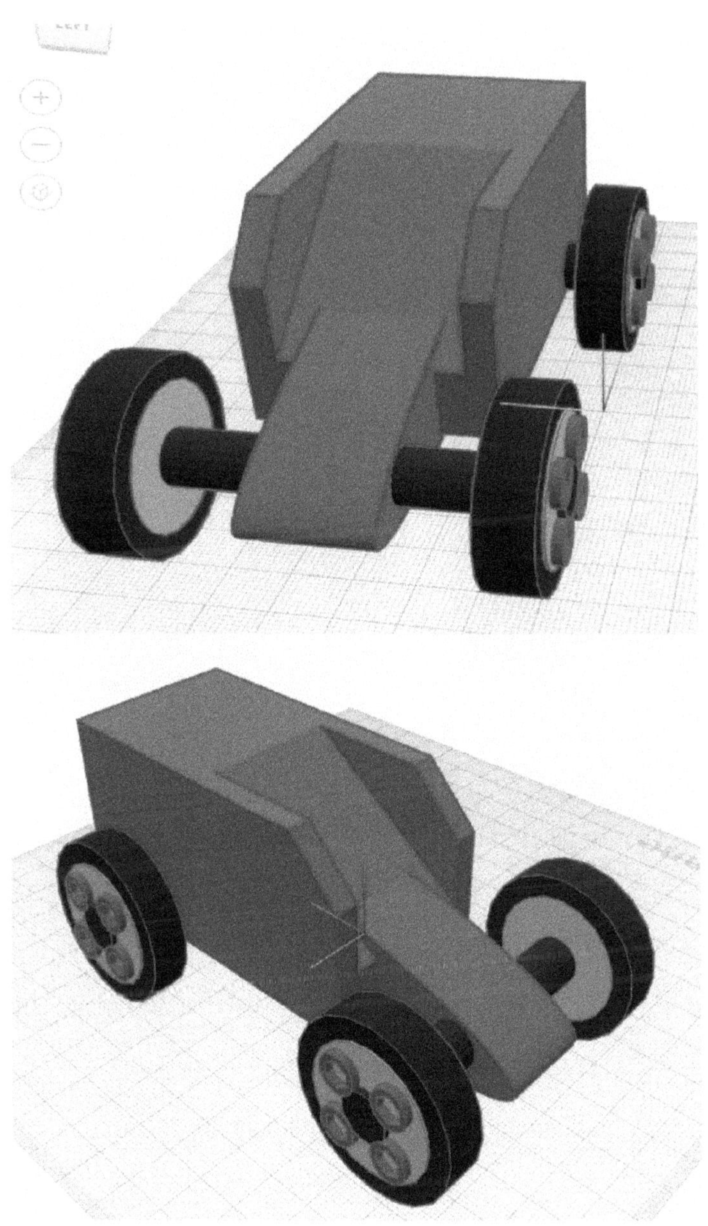

When everything looks ok, we can have all the blocks assembled and grouped together. The car is considered as completed!

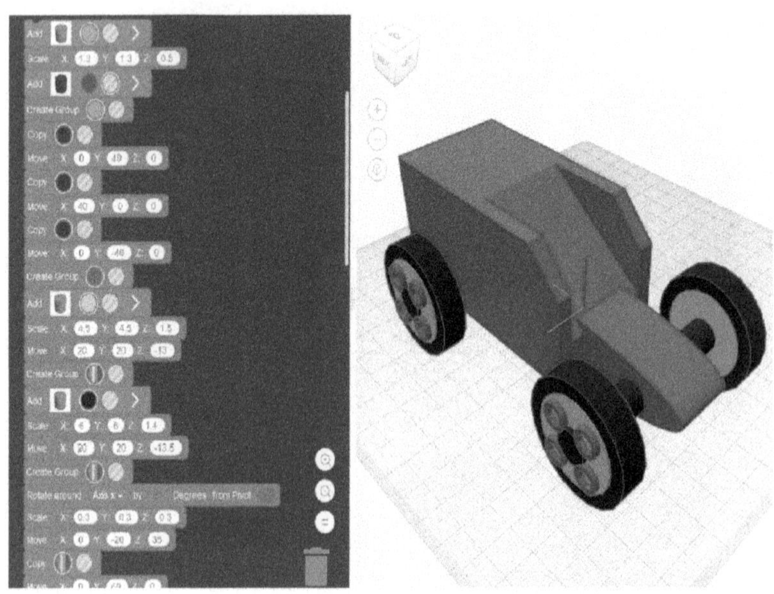

One can click Share to save the work as either PNG or animated GIF for easy sharing of the finished work.

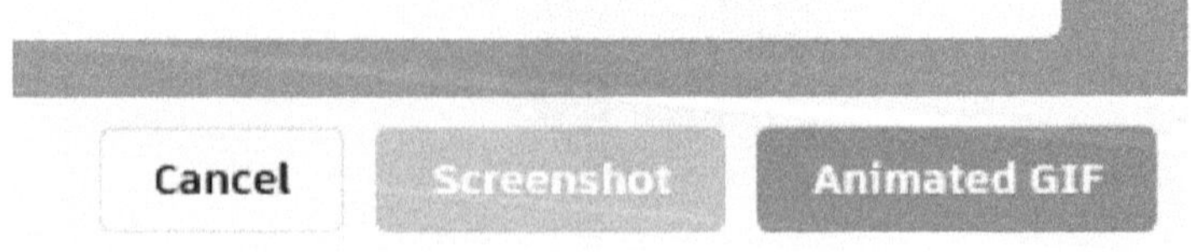

If it is screenshot then it is just a screen capture of the complete model as a still picture (without the workplane shown in the background).

If it is animated GIF then it is the complete process of building the model from start to finish. The file can be quite large.

Packaging as GIF

This may take a minute.

Your file will download automatically when completed

END OF BOOK

Please email your questions and comments to admin@Tomorrowskills.com.

www.ingramcontent.com/pod-product-compliance
Ingram Content Group UK Ltd.
Pitfield, Milton Keynes, MK11 3LW, UK
UKHW022010190726
13853UKWH00004B/1854

9 798674 918202